Teaching Music
Across the Curriculum

Valeaira Luppens • Greg Foreman

© 2011 Alfred Music
16320 Roscoe Blvd., Suite 100
P.O. Box 10003
Van Nuys, CA 91410-0003

ISBN:0-7390-8066-0
ISBN-13: 978-0-7390-8066-5

TABLE OF CONTENTS

Foreword

As educators, we understand the benefits of supporting non-musical curricular objectives, but we may feel that we can't dilute our music curriculum by spending more than a few minutes of our class time teaching or practicing non-music skills. After all, we have limited teaching time and need to use it wisely, preparing our students to achieve our district music curriculum, as well as, state and national music standards. However, by using brain-compatible teaching techniques, we can create musical meaning, as we reinforce, re-teach, and support non-music curricula, such as Communication Arts, Math, History, Social Studies, and Science within our music classrooms. We can continue to focus on our task at hand: teaching our students essential musical skills for their participation as life-long musicians and educated consumers of music, while simultaneously using common skills sets found outside our content area.

Teaching Music Across the Curriculum provides MOTIVATION by connecting students to materials, concepts, vocabulary, and ideas they're studying in their classrooms, while reinforcing the musical information they need to retain. Non-musical learners are also given an additional purpose for achieving musical goals, keeping them stimulated, regardless of any possible lack of interest in the study of "music."

Another benefit of *Teaching Music Across the Curriculum* is the promotion of TEAMWORK, helping you, the music teacher, become a key player in your school's "ensemble" by assisting your classroom teacher counterparts through the reinforcement of communication arts skills, math fluency, scientific reasoning, and historical understanding: standardized testing skills which directly reflect upon your school community and district. In many instances, *Teaching Music Across the Curriculum* may be a building goal or district initiative which we, as music teachers, are required to fulfill.

National Music Standard #8 challenges our students to achieve this goal: "Understanding relationships between music, the other arts, and disciplines outside the arts." As we are *Teaching Music Across the Curriculum*, we are supporting students' needs, assisting our counterparts in the classroom, and achieving our curricular objectives by using music as an emotional hook to inspire, create long-lasting memories, and increase critical and higher level thinking skills in our students' developing brains. We challenge you to harness the power of non-music curricular information to propel your music classes forward using the "synergy" of *Teaching Music Across the Curriculum*.

National Standards for Music Education

1. Singing, alone and with others, a varied repertoire of music.

2. Performing on instruments, alone and with others, a varied repertoire of music.

3. Improvising melodies, variations, and accompaniments.

4. Composing and arranging music within specified guidelines.

5. Reading and notating music.

6. Listening to, analyzing, and describing music.

7. Evaluating music and music performances.

8. Understanding relationships between music, the other arts, and disciples outside the arts.

9. Understanding music in relation to history and culture.

From *National Standards for Arts Education*. Copyright ©1994 by Music Educators National Conference (MENC). Used by permission. The complete National Arts Standards and additional materials relating to the standards are available from MENC.

The National Association for Music Education, 1806 Robert Fulton Drive, Reston, VA 20191

Communication Arts

One of the main reasons your principal and your classroom counterparts are eager for you to use communication arts in your music classroom is to help your students become better "test takers." Let's face it: standardized test results reflect upon your school and everything you can do to help boost those test scores will be greatly appreciated.

The following communication arts lessons can be used to teach and assess music curricular objectives, while allowing students additional "rehearsal" of the test taking vocabulary and skills, with the ultimate goal of retention of musical objectives. Being aware of the "test language" equips you, as a teacher, to increase the frequency in which students hear and process this type of language and allows you to provide concrete examples for your students, while teaching music.

Another Word

* **Italian Musical Terminology**

Time Needed:
Approximately 30 minutes

Objective::
Using a story template, students will use Italian synonyms (also called: "another word" in standardized tests) to tell a story.

Materials needed:
✂ Teacher and student worksheets
✂ Pencils

Lesson:
1. Distribute the worksheets and pencils to the students.
2. Read together as a class the Italian terminology at the end of the student worksheet.
   ♪ Provide examples, saying the words as follows:
3. Very Slow: largo
4. say "largo" very slowly, to emphasize and demonstrate the meaning of the word
   ♪ have students repeat the word, "Largo" in a very slow manner
5. Slow: adagio
6. say "adagio" slowly, but not as slowly as "largo"
   ♪ have students repeat
7. Medium speed: moderato
   ♪ say "moderato" in a medium speed
   ♪ have students repeat
8. Fast: allegro
   ♪ say "allegro" in a fast, cheerful way
   ♪ have students repeat
   ♪ tell students the word literally means "cheerful," in Italian
9. Very Fast/Quickly: presto
   ♪ say "presto" quickly
   ♪ have students repeat
10. Gradually getting faster: accelerando
    ♪ say "accelerando" beginning slowly and gradually speed up
    ♪ have students repeat

11. Gradually getting slower: ritardando
    ♪ say "ritardando" beginning quickly and gradually slowing down
    ♪ have students repeat

12. Very soft: pianissimo (*p* *p*)
    ♪ whisper "pianissimo"
    ♪ have students repeat

13. Soft: piano (*p*)
    ♪ softly say "piano"
    ♪ have students repeat

14. Medium soft: mezzo piano (*mp*)
    ♪ say "mezzo piano" in a medium soft voice
    ♪ have students repeat

15. Medium loud: mezzo forte (*mf*)
    ♪ say "mezzo forte" in a medium loud voice
    ♪ have students repeat

16. Loud: forte (*f*)
    ♪ say" forte" in a loud voice
    ♪ have students repeat

17. Very loud: fortissimo (*f* *f*)
    ♪ say "fortissimo" in a very loud voice
    ♪ have students repeat

18. Suddenly: subito
    ♪ wait a long time, and suddenly say, "subito"
    ♪ tell the class you'll cue them (like a conductor)
    ♪ wait a long time, giving the preparation quickly, and have the students say "subito" on your cue
    ♪ if the students don't follow your cue, do it again, challenging them to say the word, "subito," suddenly and together

19. Gradually getting louder: crescendo (cresc.)
    ♪ say "crescendo" gradually louder
    ♪ have students repeat

20. Gradually getting softer: decrescendo (decresc.)
    ♪ say "decrescendo" gradually softer
    ♪ have students repeat

Another Word

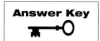

Once upon a time, Mario, the Italian sports car, was going to race in the famous "Tempo Challenge" Championship Race, just for Italian sports cars. He knew the race would be (very fast) **presto,** so he trained, got plenty of rest, had an expert "tune-up," and only used the best motor oil he could get!

On his way to the race, he noticed a fancy, red Ferrari racing his engine. Mario thought, "His engine may be (loud) **forte**, but I'm (fast) **allegro**!" So, Mario sped (quickly) **presto** past the Ferrari and (suddenly) **subito** squealed his breaks as he took his place beside the other Italian racing machines.

The other Italian sports cars revved their engines, creating a sound that was (very loud) **fortissimo**! But Mario wasn't impressed. His engine's purr was (soft) **piano**. It was so (soft) **piano**, no one even noticed him as he waited at the starting line.

The starting pistol rang above the (very loud) **fortissimo** sound of the roaring engines. (Suddenly) **subito** each car sped from the starting line, with (very loud) **fortissimo** motors roaring. The three cars in the front of the pack began to (gradually get faster) **accelerando.** Mario trying to keep up but their (very fast) **presto** pace made him look like he was going (very slow) **largo**! (Suddenly) **subito**, Mario saw an opening and he was able to position himself next to the third car. He began to (gradually get faster) **accelerando** and he passed the third car. He continued to (gradually get faster) **accelerando**, passing the second car. He could hear the (very loud) **fortissimo** sound of the cars behind him, trying to keep up!

(Suddenly), **subito** the leading car spun out of control and Mario took the lead as the crowd's cheers began to (gradually getting louder) **crescendo**. He forgot all about the cars behind him. All he could hear was the (soft) **piano** purr of his (very fast) **presto** engine as he rolled past the checkered flags and won the race!

The crowd stood and cheered, chanting "Mar-i-o" in a (medium speed) **moderato** (speed) **tempo**.

The photographers' flashbulbs were popping (quickly) **presto** as Mario drove past them in a (very slow) **largo** (speed) **tempo**. Finally, he approached the winner's circle and began to (gradually slow down) **ritardando** next to the giant, silver trophy.

Student name _____

Another Word

Directions: Fill in another word (or in this case "Italian" synonym) for the English word in the story. Extra challenge: read the story aloud using your best <u>Italian</u> accent.

Once upon a time, Mario, the Italian sports car, was going to race in the famous "Tempo Challenge" Championship Race, just for Italian sports cars. He knew the race would be (very fast) _____, so he trained, got plenty of rest, had an expert "tune-up," and only used the best motor oil he could get!

On his way to the race, he noticed a fancy, red Ferrari racing his engine. Mario thought, "His engine may be (loud) _____, but I'm (fast) _____!" So, Mario sped (quickly) _____ past the Ferrari and (suddenly) _____ squealed his breaks as he took his place beside the other Italian racing machines.

The other Italian sports cars revved their engines, creating a sound that was (very loud) _____! But Mario wasn't impressed. His engine's purr was (soft) _____. It was so (soft) _____, no one even noticed him as he waited at the starting line.

The starting pistol rang above the (very loud) _____ sound of the roaring engines. (Suddenly) _____ each car sped from the starting line, with (very loud) _____ motors roaring. The three cars in the front of the pack began to (gradually get faster) _____. Mario tried to keep up, but their (very fast) _____ pace made him look like he was going (very slow) _____! (Suddenly) _____, Mario saw an opening and he was able to position himself next to the third car. He began to (gradually get faster) _____ and he passed the third car. He continued to (gradually get faster) _____, passing the second car. He could hear the (very loud) _____ sound of the cars behind him, trying to keep up!

(Suddenly), _____ the leading car spun out of control and Mario took the lead as the crowd's cheers began to (gradually getting louder) _____. He forgot all about the cars behind him. All he could hear was the (soft) _____ purr of his (very fast) _____ engine as he rolled past the checkered flags and won the race!

The crowd stood and cheered, chanting "Mar-i-o" in a (medium speed) _____ (speed) _____. The photographers' flashbulbs were popping (quickly) _____ as Mario drove past them in a (very slow)_____ (speed) _____. Finally, he approached the winner's circle and began to (gradually slow down) _____ next to the giant, silver trophy.

Common Italian Terminology (tempo and dynamics)

Speed: **tempo**

Very Slow: **largo**

Slow: **adagio**

Medium speed: **moderato**

Fast: **allegro**

Very Fast/Quickly: **presto**

Gradually getting faster: **accelerando**

Gradually getting slower: **ritardando**

Very soft: **pianissimo** (*pp*)

Soft: **piano** (*p*)

Medium soft: **mezzo piano** (*mp*)

Medium loud: **mezzo forte** (*mf*)

Loud: **forte** (*f*)

Very loud: **fortissimo** (*ff*)

Suddenly: **subito**

Gradually getting louder: **crescendo** (cresc.)

Gradually getting softer: **decrescendo** (decresc.)

Amazing Acronyms

★ **Correlating communication arts and music**

Time Needed:
Approximately 30 minutes

Objective:
The students will be able to create an acronym for the lines and spaces in both the treble and bass clefs.

Materials Needed:
✂ Student worksheets
✂ Pencils

Lesson:
1. Review the line and space notes in the treble and bass clefs.
2. Pass out worksheets and pencils.
3. Read the definition of an acronym to the class which is located on the student worksheet.
4. As a class, write an acronym for each of the clefs on the board.
5. Divide the class into groups of two or three.
6. Instruct each group to create their own unique music staff acronyms on the back of their worksheets.
   ♪ If you use colorful paper for the final draft, this assignment can be cut into creative shapes and placed on a bulletin board. Students love to see their own work displayed and it will further reinforce the note naming strategy.
   ♪ This assignment can also be written in their journals.

Amazing Acronyms

An acronym is formed when each initial letter, or a small group of letters, make up the basis and meaning of a compound term. Each beginning letter stands for a specific word such as NASA which is an acronym for "National Aeronautics and Space Administration," or DARE which stands for "Drug Abuse Resistance Education."

Acronyms can be used as a learning tool for the retention of information. Most students know that FACE can be used to identify the space notes in the treble clef and that **EGBDF** "**E**very **G**ood **B**oy **D**eserves **F**udge," or "**E**very **G**ood **B**oy **D**oes **F**ine," or "**E**mpty **G**arbage **B**efore **D**ad **F**lips," or "**E**lvis's **G**uitar **B**roke **D**own **F**riday" are acronyms for the lines in the treble clef. Examples of the acronym, **ACEG**, used to remember the letter names in the bass clef, include "**A**ll **C**ars **E**at **G**as" or "**A**ll **C**ows **E**at **G**rass." Popular acronyms for the lines of the bass clef, **GBDFA**, include "**G**ood **B**oys **D**o **F**ine **A**lways," or "**G**irls **B**uy **D**onuts **F**riday **A**fternoon." On the back of this paper, create your own unique music staff acronyms. Remember, the choices must be in these patterns:

(Treble Clef Lines): **E G B D F**

(Treble Clef Spaces): **F A C E**

(Bass Clef Lines): **G B D F A**

(Bass Clef Spaces): **A C E G**

Student name(s) _____

Treble Clef Lines:

E _____ G _____ B _____ D _____F_____

Treble Clef Spaces:

F_____ A _____C_____E_____

Bass Clef Lines:

G _____ B _____D _____F_____ A _____

Bass Clef Spaces:

A _____ C _____E _____G_____

Bonus: Create additional acronyms for the treble and bass clefs in the space below or make a drawing of your favorite acronym(s)!

Construction Zone

★ **Correlating music and communication arts testing skills**

Time Needed:
Approximately 30 to 40 minutes

Objective:
Using the worksheets, students will practice writing "constructed responses," a common form of written answer in standardized testing.

Materials Needed:
✂ Teacher and student worksheets
✂ Pencils

Lesson:
1. Pass out the worksheets and pencils to the students.

2. **Constructed Responses** require students to supply, rather than select, an appropriate answer or response. (These are *not* opinion questions.) The response should include supporting details and/or examples.

3. Usually, constructed responses are graded using a "scoring guide" or "rubric." Points are awarded if the necessary information is included, but points usually aren't deducted if additional information is given (in other words, you can give more information than you think is necessary).

4. **Answer Key** for Constructed Responses (answers may vary slightly):

   ♪ I expect a violin to play higher pitches than a string bass because violins have shorter, thinner strings and smaller bodies and a string bass has longer, thicker strings and a larger body.

   ♪ A piano keyboard is similar to a number line because piano keyboard pitches become higher as you move from left to right. Similarly, the number line's value becomes higher as you move from left to right. The opposite is also true, the pitches become lower as you move from right to left on a piano and the number values become lower as you move from right to left.

   ♪ A clarinet and an oboe are different because the clarinet is larger, plays a wider range than the oboe, uses a single reed, does not use vibrato, and is a B♭ instrument. In contrast, the oboe is smaller, uses a double reed, has nearly a three octave range, uses vibrato, and is a C instrument.

   ♪ Musicians use Italian terminology because many of the important early composers in the "Renaissance era" were Italian, so they started the tradition of using Italian terms to describe musical directions for performers. Since many standard pieces of music are performed world-wide, Italian terminology has been adopted as a common language for musical directions.

Student name _____

Construction Zone

Constructed Responses are written questions found on standardized tests. The more you practice these types of answers, the better test taker you'll become. Here's an example of a musical, constructed response:

Q. Why is the saxophone considered a "Woodwind" instrument, even though it is made of brass?

A. The saxophone is considered a "Woodwind" instrument because it uses a reed on a mouthpiece to create the sound. Brass instruments create their sound by buzzing lips in a mouthpiece. (Notice the response restated the question and didn't initially refer to the saxophone as "it." The answer also used the terms reed, mouthpiece, and buzzing to demonstrate knowledge of instrument tone production. The answer uses complete sentences, punctuation, and capitalization at the beginning of sentences.)

Read the paragraph and use the information to help you construct your responses to the questions:

Violins, violas, cellos, string basses, and harps belong to an instrument group known as the "string family." The vibrating strings transfer their sound to the bodies of the instruments, to produce their unique sound. Small instruments produce higher pitches because of the shorter, thinner strings and smaller bodies; while the larger instruments produce lower pitches because their strings are longer, thicker and their bodies are larger. Most of the orchestral instruments, with the exception of the harp, use a bow, drawn across the strings to cause the strings to vibrate. Sometimes strings are plucked, like the harp, to cause it to vibrate and produce sound.

 1. Why do you expect a violin to play higher pitches than a string bass?

 _____

 _____

 _____

Have you ever noticed piano keyboards and number lines have things in common? Piano keyboard pitches become higher as you move from left to right. Similarly, the number line's value becomes higher as you move from left to right. The opposite is also true, the pitches become lower as you move from right to left on a piano and the number values become lower as you move from right to left, also. Piano keyboards and number lines are both horizontal, but a piano keyboard has only 88 keys and a number line can continue to infinite. The next time you use a number line or a piano, notice how organized the number line and piano keys both are!

2. How is a piano keyboard similar to a number line?

_____

_____

_____

The clarinet and the oboe are both woodwind instruments because the clarinet and oboe are both made of wood, wind is blown into them, and they use reeds to create their sounds. They have many differences including size, reeds, vibrato, and pitch. The clarinet is larger, plays a wider range than the oboe, uses a single reed, does not use vibrato, and is a B♭ instrument. In contrast, the oboe is smaller, uses a double reed, has nearly a three octave range, uses vibrato, and is a C instrument.

3. What are the differences between a clarinet and an oboe?

_____

_____

_____

Have you ever wondered why you see foreign language words in musical scores, reviews, and program notes? During the "Renaissance era," many of the important early composers were Italian, so they started the tradition of using Italian terms to describe musical directions for performers. Since many standard pieces of music are performed world-wide, Italian terminology has been adopted as a common language for musical directions, although many directions are now written in English or translated into the native languages of individual countries.

4. Why do musicians use Italian terminology?

_____

_____

_____

Effectively Using Picture Books

★ **Reading to your students for pleasure and information**

Time Needed:
Approximately 20 minutes (varies according to book length)

Objective:
Using a picture book, read aloud to your students while discussing content as a class.

Materials Needed:
✂ Picture Book (Picture books draw students' attention even in upper grades.)

Lesson:
1. "Picture Books" provide opportunities for you to:
   - ♪ discuss vocabulary (both musical and non-musical)
   - ♪ build students' **"Schema"** (their framework or understanding of specific topics)
   - ♪ create historical connections, using apparel, hair styles, architecture, etc.
   - ♪ entertain students through interesting, vivid stories about musicians/musical topics

2. Before reading the book, show the book cover to the class and ask them to make predictions of:
   - ♪ "What do you think this book will be about?"
   - ♪ "What is one of the first events they think will happen in the book?" (**Prediction** is a skill used by good readers and will help to get students involved in the text.)

3. Throughout the book, include a few "predictions" of what will happen next from your class. This will:
   - ♪ keep them involved
   - ♪ check for understanding

4. As you read the picture book, show the pictures of each page BEFORE you read the text, then show the picture again.
   - ♪ This will allow the students to form an accurate visual image while you're reading.
   - ♪ Again, this helps to involve students in the text.

5. As you are reading, ask questions about the text.
   - ♪ Ask students about their opinions and prior knowledge to connect them more deeply with the story and check for understanding.

6. Use interesting voices and inflections to interpret the story in an imaginative way.

7. Picture books can be used as part of or as a complete lesson on instruments, musicians, composers, or musical styles. The only limit is availability of books.
   - ♪ If the book is not readily available from your school's library, books can also be borrowed from other school libraries if you plan ahead and ask your library personnel to locate them.

♪ Books can be purchased from local new/used bookstores or online by typing in a search for: "Children's Books Elementary Music Curriculum."

8. Picture books are also a great way to calm classes after recess, fire drill, or other transitional events.

 ♪ refocuses students on music study

 ♪ quiets talking from prior loud activities

 ♪ easily obtained, pro-active classroom management tool

9. Additional follow-up activities

 ♪ write a book review/report

 ♪ illustrate a "new version" of the book (class or individual project)

 ♪ students can retell the story, remembering the order of events

 ♪ students can "act" the story as a mini-play

 ♪ students can take turns re-reading the story to the class, using expression and articulation

Jazzy Journaling

★ **Correlating music with writing skills**

Time Needed:
Variable

Objective:
The students will be able to correctly notate their musical learning experiences in a journal.

Materials Needed:
✂ Journal (i.e. a notebook, or a three ring paper binder filled with notebook paper)
✂ Pencils

Lesson:
Journaling can be effectively implemented into the music classroom. Not only can it be utilized to increase the student's vocabulary, it can successfully impact the concepts taught within the music classroom ranging from dynamic and tempo terms to rudimentary vocabulary terms and symbols. Listed below are a few suggestions you may wish to put into practice for your students' journal. The possibilities are limitless! The journal can also be graded on spelling and correct punctuation if you so choose.

1. Have the students write a brief summary of a movie they viewed in music (i.e. *Peter and the Wolf*).
2. Instruct the students to write down musical terms and symbols as you learn them throughout the year. Examples:
   ♪ **Forte** is an Italian dynamic term which means loud. The symbol for forte looks like this: f
   ♪ **Allegro** is an Italian tempo term which means fast
   ♪ A **flat** lowers a note one half step. The symbol for a flat is ♭.
3. Journaling can also be used as a review or a comprehension check. For example:
   ♪ Today we learned about key signatures which can be found directly after the clef symbol at the beginning of a piece of music. The top number indicates how many beats there will be in a measure. The bottom number tells what type of note will receive one beat. In $\frac{3}{4}$ time, there are three beats per measure and a quarter note receives one beat.
4. Journaling is an effective tool for the students to write their reactions, feelings, criticisms, and or reviews relating to the music or topics being covered in the classroom.
5. Journaling can also be used to promote note-taking skills when learning new material.
6. Hint! Before you start journaling, allocate an area to house the journals. Also, the first time you use the journals, be sure the student's and teacher's class name is clearly written on upper right hand corner of the booklet. A journal can be used throughout the class period, or for just a few minutes at the beginning or end of class.

Maelzel's Marvelous Metronome

★ **Correlating music and creative writing**

Time Needed:
Approximately 30 to 40 minutes

Objective:
The students will be able to write a creative story about a metronome and three disassociated items found in a paper sack.

Materials Needed:
✕ Teacher and student worksheets
✕ Lined paper and pencils
✕ Metronome
✕ Paper bag containing a rock, a child's toy, and a spoon (any variable item may be used)

Lesson:
1. Pass out the metronome worksheets and read together as a class.

2. Ask three different students to come up to the front of the classroom. To add a little suspense, one student at a time will remove an item from the sack (a rock, a child's toy, and a spoon).

3. Place the metronome and the three items in an area easily seen by the students, and then instruct the students to write a creative story based on these articles. The story must contain the following guidelines:

   ♪ Three paragraphs using complete sentences and proper grammar

   ♪ Each of the items taken from the sack must be mentioned in the story along with the metronome

4. Encourage the students to be creative.

5. Distribute lined paper and pencils to the students.

6. After the papers have been completed, you may want to have some or all of the students read their stories to the class.

7. These stories may also be housed in their journals.

Maelzel's Marvelous Metronome

Maelzel's marvelous metronome was originally invented to inform musicians of the exact tempo for which a piece of music should be played. The first metronomes were triangular in shape, but today they come in many different sizes and shapes; even tiny digital boxes! The metronome has a clock-like mechanism that has a double pendulum which ticks steady, even tempos. It can be set on a variety of speeds by raising and lowering the weight up and down ranging from very slow to very fast. If you look closely at the beginning of many classical works, you will see the letters MM followed by a number. The letters, MM, stand for Maelzel's Metronome, and the numbers indicate the speed of the tempo (the number of beats per minute). Metronomes are also used for rehearsal because the steady beat can help musicians keep their rhythms even.

Shh! Here's a secret most people don't know! Maelzel didn't actually invent the first metronome. Dietrich Nikolaus Winkel, of Amsterdam, did in 1812! In 1816, Maelzel made the type of metronome that we still use today!

Musical Spelling Bee

★ **Correlating music with spelling skills**

Time Needed:
Variable

Objective:
The students will be able to correctly spell commonly used musical terms.

Materials Needed:
✂ Student spelling sheets

Lesson:
1. Inform the students that they are going to be participating in a Musical Spelling Bee.
2. Distribute the spelling sheets to the students.
   - ♪ allow students to study in small groups, pairs, or alone for five minute intervals
   - ♪ provide in-class study time during several consecutive class periods
   - ♪ if possible, post the study sheet on your school's web page (this will increase at-home study time and draw students to your other web links)
   - ♪ to create meaning for the words, say and have students repeat the word and their pronunciation — see the lesson *Another Word* (synonym)
3. Allow the students approximately five minutes to review the musical spelling sheets during the class period of "The Bee."
4. After the review, instruct the students to lay the study sheets face down on the floor. Have all the students stand.
   - ♪ Select a student to begin.
   - ♪ State the spelling word, then use it in a sentence so the students get a review of what the word means. (ex. **Forte**. Because the music was marked **forte**, the students knew they would have to sing loudly.)
   - ♪ Have the student repeat the word before they spell it.
   - ♪ If the student spells the word correctly, he/she will remain standing; otherwise the child must sit down and the word is repeated for the next student.
   - ♪ Continue the game until only one student remains standing (or several in case of a tie).
   - ♪ You may choose to create a list with simpler words for younger grade levels.
   - ♪ These words can also be used as "Word Wall" vocabulary (words introduced within various lessons, which you post on your classroom walls). Just remember to have students face away from the word wall or remove the words before your "bee."

SPELLING BEE LIST

tempo	grave	adagio
lento	moderato	andante
vivace	allegro	presto
ritardando	accelerando	dynamics
piano	mezzo piano	pianissimo
forte	mezzo forte	fortissimo
crescendo	decrescendo	diminuendo
symbols	tie	slur
phrase	accent	staccato
legato	fermata	sharp
flat	natural	repeat sign
time signature	meter signature	eighth note
quarter note	half note	whole note
lyrics	composer	conductor
instruments	strings	woodwinds
brass	percussion	keyboards

Oxymorons

★ **Correlating music with writing skills**

Time Needed:
Approximately 1 class period

Objective:
The students will be able to correctly identify an oxymoron.

Materials Needed:
✂ Student song sheets
✂ Student worksheets
✂ Pencils

Lesson:
1. Discuss the definition of an oxymoron:

   ♪ An oxymoron is a combination of contradictory words such as deafening silence or jumbo shrimp.

2. Teach the "Oxymorons" song (sung to the Dutch folk tune: "Sarasponda")

3. Instruct the students to write down all the oxymorons found within the song.

   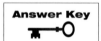

   ♪ Awfully good

   ♪ Pretty ugly

   ♪ Inside out

   ♪ Upside down

   ♪ Bitter sweet

   ♪ Clearly confused

   ♪ Clever fools

   ♪ Alone together

   ♪ Now and then

4. Instruct the students to write a "rap" using the same set of oxymorons.

   ♪ The rap must have at least 4 couplets (8 lines)

   ♪ Each line should have approximately 8 syllables

   ♪ The last word in each couplet must rhyme

   ♪ The students may work individually, or in groups of 2 or 4.

Oxymorons

Lyrics by Valeaira Luppens

Dutch Folk Tune "Sarasponda"

Soprano / Piano

Ox - y - mo - rons! Ox - y - mo - rons are so con - tra - dic - to - ry! Ox - y -

mo - rons! Ox - y - mo - rons they just love to dis - a - gree! They're

aw - ful - ly good! And pret - ty ug - ly, too! They're

Oxymorons

Write a list of all the oxymorons found within the song:

_____

_____

_____

_____

_____

_____

_____

_____

On the back of this worksheet, write a "rap" using the same set of oxymorons. Please include the following:

• Your rap must have at least four couplets (eight lines)

• Each line should have approximately eight syllables

• The last word in each couplet must rhyme

Tricky Anagrams

★ **Correlating language, spelling, and music**

Time Needed:
Approximately 30 minutes

Objective:
The students will be able to correctly identify the music terms listed on their worksheets by unscrambling the anagrams.

Materials Needed:
✂ Teacher and student worksheets
✂ Pencils

Lesson:
1. Distribute student worksheets and pencils.
2. Discuss the definition of an anagram:
   ♪ An anagram is a word formed by rearranging the letters of another word.
3. Explain that each of the anagrams listed on the student worksheet can be formed into a word relating to music.
4. Place an example on the board:
   ♪ beast – beats (The counts found in each measure of music.)
5. This activity can be completed individually or in small groups. Determine which would be best for your students.
6.

   ♪ par – rap
   ♪ charm – march
   ♪ note – tone
   ♪ cork – rock
   ♪ riot – trio
   ♪ Oslo – solo
   ♪ harps – sharp
   ♪ supersonic – percussion
   ♪ phonic – Chopin
   ♪ café – face

Student name _____

Tricky Anagrams

An anagram is a word made by rearranging the letters of another word. Did you know that solving anagrams can actually help your spelling? It forces you to pay better attention to how the words are spelled! See if you can solve the music related anagrams below! (Feel free to use the hints!)

1. par: _____
(Hint! A popular form of vocal music where the emphasis is on speaking rather than singing.)

2. charm: _____
(Hint! Music, usually in duple or quadruple meter, often used in parades for bands.)

3. note: _____
(Hint! The pitch of the note)

4. cork: _____
(Hint! A form of popular music often derived from country, folk or blues which is generally performed on electronically amplified instruments with strongly emphasized rhythms.)

5. riot: _____
(Hint! A group of three instrumental or vocal musicians performing together.)

6. Oslo: _____
(Hint! An instrumental or vocal performance by an individual person.)

7. harps: _____
(Hint! This symbol raises the pitch of the note ½ step.)

8. supersonic: _____
(Hint! One of the families of the orchestra.)

9. phonic: _____
(Hint! A famous pianist/composer who was born in Poland, but left at the age of 20 to live in France.)

10. café: _____
(Hint! The letters in this word spell out the names of the pitches in the treble clef.)

Tech It!

★ **Correlating music with communication arts, through technology**

Time Needed:
Various

Objective:
Students will be introduced to free, technology resources to support music and non-musical curricular objectives.

Materials Needed:
✂ Computer
✂ Internet Connection
✂ Projector (optional)

Lesson:
1. Free, technology resources are available to help your students with both musical and non-musical projects. We can easily make them aware of these tools by demonstrating their uses in our music classrooms and, if possible, create links on our web pages or blogs so they will have quick access for homework and projects.

2. The following list is a reproducible page (for you or your students) of links which can support multiple curricula, including your music lessons, while building student vocabulary, providing help with song writing, translating foreign languages, and supplying maps and copyright free images for creating blogs, videos, or slide presentations about specific topics, including music.

Tech It

1. **Google Maps** (maps.google.com) can be used to quickly find geographical regions, countries, or continents related to specific composers, styles of music, or historical events.

2. **Lexipedia** (lexipedia.com), **Snappy Words** (snappywords.com) and **Visuwords** (visuwords.com) are free, visual online dictionaries and thesauruses. All three web sites provide visual "**web**" or "**cluster**," graphic organizers used to generate ideas about a concept, theme, or topic. To use, type a word in the search field to "web" antonyms, synonyms, and similar words. When your cursor is placed over individual words, definition boxes appear. Each webbed word is color coded, to identify its use as a noun, verb, adjective, or adverb. When you want to explore a related word, double click on that word and the site will form a new word web. Here are possible music applications:

   - Composer (types of composers and musical compositions)
   - Conductor (note the many types of "conductors")
   - Music (types of music; related words)
   - Musical Instruments (types of instruments, forms)
   - Singer (type of singers; vocal classifications)
   - Tempo (Italian terms; synonyms)

3. **Morguefile** (morgue.com) sounds gruesome, but has great, copyright-free, music related images. These images can be used for web pages, blogs, and school or home projects. Additional sites for pictures include: **Pics4Learning** (pics4learning.com) and **American Memory** (memory.loc.gov) from the Library of Congress.

4. **School Tube** (schooltube.com) and **Teacher Tube** (teachertube.com) allows teachers and schools to create and share their work. Each video is reviewed before it is posted, to insure safe "surfing."

   Search Engines for students:
   - **Ask for Kids** (askkids.com)
   - **Cyber Sleuth** (cybersleuth-kids.com)
   - **Dib Dab Doo** (dibdabdoo.com)
   - **Fact Monster** (factmonster.com)
   - **Famhoo**: a family friendly search engine (famhoo.com)
   - **KidRex** (kidrex.org)

- **OneKey**: the kid safe search engine (onekey.com)
- **Schoolr** (schoolr.com)
- **Sort Fix** (sortfix.com)
- **Sweet Search**: a search engine for students (sweetsearch.com)

5. **Translate Google** (translate.google.com) allows students to translate foreign languages into English or English text into foreign languages. This can be useful when trying to understand Italian musical terminology or translating lyrics of a foreign language song.

6. **Write Express** (rhymer.com) is a great tool for aspiring lyricists and poets, providing a free, rhyming dictionary with a drop down arrow to select:
   - End Rhymes
   - Last Syllable Rhymes
   - Double Rhymes
   - Beginning Rhymes
   - First Syllable Rhymes

History

Content Standard #9 of the *National Standards for Music Education* states that our students are to achieve the goal of "Understanding music in relation to history and culture." Facing this complex mission, we are confronted with the task of creating fun, meaningful ways to build connections to composers, musical time periods, and other cultures' musical languages.

We can accomplish this by relating composers to their famous, non-musical contemporaries, as well as capturing students' attention by inserting additional communication arts and standardized testing practice within lessons, giving the activities greater purpose and intrinsic motivation (especially for non-musical learners).

The following group of lessons will explore and demonstrate additional ways to reach students through cross-curricular teaching methods, by practicing the use of the Venn diagram, story writing, fact classification, geography, and language skills.

1732: Birth of Two "Fathers"

★ **Comparing George Washington to Franz Joseph Haydn**

Time Needed:
Approximately 30 minutes

Objective:
Using a Venn diagram, students will compare and contrast the differences between two, important historical figures.

Materials Needed:
✂ Teacher and student worksheets
✂ Pencils

Lesson:
1. Ask students to tell you everything they know (or think they know) about George Washington.
   - ♪ First president of the United States
   - ♪ Famous myth—he chopped down a cherry tree
   - ♪ (answers will vary, depending upon prior knowledge)
2. Ask students to tell you everything they know (or think they know) about Franz Joseph Haydn.
   - ♪ Composer
   - ♪ (answers will vary, depending upon prior knowledge)
3. Distribute student worksheets and pencils.
4. Tell students:
   - ♪ "Read the short biographies of George Washington and Franz Joseph Haydn.
   - ♪ They were both born in the same year and were very famous men.
   - ♪ After you have finished reading their stories, identify the things they have in common and list those things in the center (the intersecting area) of the Venn diagram, on your worksheet.
   - ♪ Next, list the things different about the two men within the area outside of the intersecting area.
   - ♪

5.

George Washington
*Born to a wealthy
  family
*Father of our Country
*First president of the
  U.S.A.
*Tall and had brown hair

*Powdered his hair
*Wore tights, a long coat,
  and buckle shoes
*Born the same year

Franz Joseph Haydn
*Born to a middle class
  family
*Father of the Symphony
*Father of the String
  Quartet
*Short and bald
  (wore a wig)

INK

1732: Birth of Two Fathers

George Washington was born on February 22, 1732 to a rich, plantation family in Virginia and later became the first President of the United States in 1789. Because he helped to create our system of government, he became known as "George Washington: Father of Our Country." He was 6'2" tall and had brown hair, but wore white powder on it, since that was the custom of the time. He also wore tights, a long coat, and buckle shoes. Many people have heard the story of young George chopping down his father's cherry tree and when his father asked him about it, he replied, "I cannot tell a lie." That story is thought to have been invented after Washington died in 1799.

Franz Joseph Haydn was born on March 3, 1732. His father was a wagon wheel builder and his mother had been a cook for a royal family in Austria. Mr. Haydn became known as "Father of the Symphony" and "Father of the String Quartet" because he made important contributions to both types of music. He was a very famous composer in Europe when he died in 1809. Haydn was a short man and wore a long coat, tights, and buckle shoes, which was the style in the 18th Century (1700–1800). He also wore a "white, powdered wig," but he was actually bald.

George Washington and Franz Joseph Haydn probably never met, but were both born in the same year. Using the "Venn Diagram," write the facts that are the same in the center of the diagram and the facts that are different in the sides of the diagram.

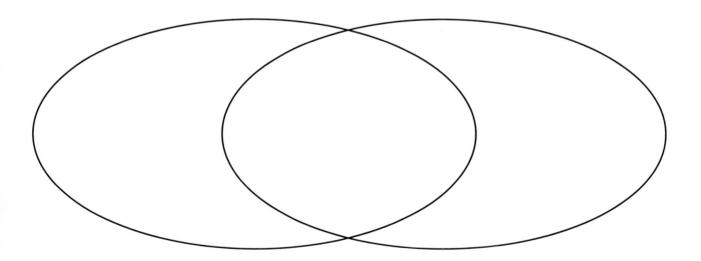

Brahms' Story Starter

★ **Correlating music, history and language skills**

Time Needed:
Approximately 30 minutes

Objective:
Using the facts listed on the worksheet, students will be able to complete a story about Brahms.

Materials Needed:
✂ Teacher and student worksheets
✂ Pencils

Lesson:
1. Discuss the job skills required for a news reporter:

   ♪ needs to gather facts

   ♪ selects ideas to include in the news story which are the most important

   ♪ creates a well-written, understandable news story people will want to read or listen to on the radio, television, or internet

2. Pass out the student worksheets and pencils.

3. Read the directions as a class, assigning the students the task of creating an interesting news story.

4. Grammar, spelling, and punctuation are important!

Brahms' Story Starter

You are a reporter for a local news office. Listed below are facts about a famous composer named Johannes Brahms. Use these facts to finish the story on the next page. Please use correct grammar, spelling, and punctuation in your story, which includes at least five of the following facts:

- His father discovered at a young age that Brahms was gifted at playing the piano.

- Brahms started composing (writing) music at age twelve.

- In 1853, he met Robert and Clara Schumann (both well known musicians at the time) who thought he was a musical genius. Robert sent Brahms to Leipzig where he found two publishers to promote his work and met another great musician/composer named Hector Berlioz.

- In 1862, Brahms moved to Vienna where he lived for the rest of his life.

- Brahms wrote a large variety of music including several symphonies, piano concertos, two volumes of Hungarian Dances, waltzes, rhapsodies and chamber music.

- Brahms never got married.

- Brahms' clothes were always clean, but outdated.

- The composer only had a few close friends.

- Brahms died when he was 64, on April 3, 1897.

Johannes Brahms

When Johannes Brahms was born in Hamburg, Germany on May 7, 1833, he probably looked like any other baby. What would his family have thought if they had known that their child would become one of the most famous musicians in the world? When Johannes was quite young, his father discovered that _____

_____

_____

_____

_____

_____

_____

_____

_____

_____

_____

_____

Classical Classification!

★ **Categorize Composers within Classical Music Time Periods**

Time Needed:
Approximately 30 minutes

Objective:
Using a spreadsheet, students will classify composers from different time periods by birth and death dates.

Materials Needed:
✂ Teacher and student sheets
✂ Pencils

Lesson:
1. Distribute the worksheets and ask the students to classify the alphabetical list of composers to their correct time periods.

2. Composers are generally classified in the period where they lived most of their adult life (so their death date is more important than their birth date, when classifying them into a musical history period).

3. Notice that some composers were so important; their death dates were used to end the musical history period in which they are best known.

4. To **classify** something or someone, is to group them with similar things or people. Musicians *classify* music and composers into specific categories by time periods, styles, and instrumentation.

5.

Baroque 1600–1750	Classical 1750–1825	Romantic 1825–1900	Modern 1900–present
Johann Sebastian Bach 1685–1750	Ludwig van Beethoven 1770–1827	Georges Bizet 1838–1875	Leonard Bernstein 1918–1990
George Frideric Handel 1685–1759	Franz Joseph Haydn 1732–1809	Alexander Borodin 1833–1887	Benjamin Britten 1913–1976
Henry Purcell 1659–1695	Wolfgang Amadeus Mozart 1756–1791	Johannes Brahms 1833–1897	John Cage 1912–1992
Domenico Scarlatti 1685–1757		Frédéric Chopin 1810–1849	Aaron Copland 1900–1990
Georg Philipp Telemann 1681–1767		Franz Liszt 1811–1886	George Gershwin 1898–1937
Antonio Vivaldi 1678–1741		Felix Mendelssohn 1809–1847	Charles Ives 1874–1954
		Robert Schumann 1810–1856	Sergei Prokofiev 1891–1953
		Clara Schumann 1819–1896	Dmitri Shostakovich 1906–1975
		Johann Strauss Jr. 1825–1899	Igor Stravinsky 1882–1971
		Piotr Ilyich Tchaikovsky 1840–1893	

Classical Classification!

Review this list of composers and classify them in their correct music history period. Remember, their musical careers were usually more important when they are/were adults, so their death dates will help to indicate which period is the correct one.

Johann Sebastian Bach 1685–1750
Ludwig van Beethoven 1770–1827
Leonard Bernstein 1918–1990
Georges Bizet 1838–1875
Alexander Borodin 1833–1887
Johannes Brahms 1833–1897
Benjamin Britten 1913–1976
John Cage 1912–1992
Frédéric Chopin 1810–1849
Aaron Copland 1900–1990
George Gershwin 1898–1937
George Frideric Handel 1685–1759
Franz Joseph Haydn 1732–1809
Charles Ives 1874–1954
Franz Liszt 1811–1886
Felix Mendelssohn 1809–1847
Wolfgang Amadeus Mozart 1756–1791
Sergei Prokofiev 1891–1953
Henry Purcell 1659–1695
Domenico Scarlatti 1685–1757
Robert Schumann 1810–1856
Clara Schumann 1819–1896
Dmitri Shostakovich 1906–1975
Johann Strauss Jr. 1825–1899
Igor Stravinsky 1882–1971
Piotr Ilyich Tchaikovsky 1840–1893
Georg Philipp Telemann 1681–1767
Antonio Vivaldi 1678–1741

Student name _____

Classical Classification!

Baroque 1600–1750	Classical 1750–1825	Romantic 1825–1900	Modern 1900–present

Gioacchino Rossini

★ Correlating music, history and language arts

Time Needed:
Approximately 30 minutes

Objective:
The students will be able to correctly identify the homophones in the biography of Gioacchino Rossini.

Materials Needed:
✂ Teacher and student worksheets
✂ Pencils
✂ Optional: CD of Rossini's music

Lesson:
1. Review the definition of homophones:

   ♪ Homophones are two or more words that sound alike, but are usually spelled differently.

2. Distribute student worksheets and pencils.

3. Read the biography together as a class.

4. Instruct the students to reread the material and circle all the homophones found within the biography.

   ♪ You may wish to play an excerpt of Rossini's music such as *The Barber of Seville* while they complete the worksheet.

5.

   ♪ sent

   ♪ son

   ♪ to

   ♪ where

   ♪ wrote

   ♪ wait

   ♪ led

   ♪ for

   ♪ no

   ♪ write

   ♪ marry

   ♪ their

Student name _____

Gioacchino Rossini

Homophones are two or more words that sound alike, but are usually spelled differently. Circle the correct homophone in the biography below.

Gioacchino Rossini was born in 1792, in Pesaro, Italy. When he was young, he was so handsome the townspeople called him "the angel." His childhood was troubled though because his father had been (cent, sent) to prison, resulting from his political beliefs. During this period, his mother worked part-time, singing in a number of opera houses. Gioacchino was forced to live with a pork butcher until his father was finally released from jail. When the family was reunited, his father, who was the town trumpeter, started teaching his (son, sun) (to, two) play the french horn. Rossini also took vocal lessons from the village priest. Later they moved to Bologna (where wear) he eventually became a student at the Liceo Musicale. He studied the cello, piano, singing and counterpoint. Rossini loved both composition and the opera. He (rote, wrote) his first opera when he was only a teenager. As an adult, Rossini was very successful. He married a famous singer named Isabella Colbran. Rossini composed a series of operas, but had the irritating habit of tending to (wait, weight) until the last minute to finish his compositions. This (led, lead) to many traumatic moments (for, four) everyone as the deadline for the shows drew near. Although he enjoyed various types of music, he is best known for his operas, especially *The Barber of Seville* and *Cinderella*. In 1829, he suddenly decided he (know, no) longer wanted to (write, right) operas. When his first wife died, he decided to (merry, marry) again and moved to Paris. He and his wife enjoyed entertaining (there, their, they're) friends at home. Not only did they serve the finest food in Paris, Rossini enjoyed performing his music on the piano, and being a witty host. His house was filled with the sounds of laughter! He spent the remainder of his life living in Paris, writing scores of songs and piano and instrumental pieces. Rossini was a superstitious man, who ironically enough, died on Friday the 13th in 1868. He left his vast fortune to open a conservatory of music in his home town and to fund a home for aged and infirm singers in France.

Similes

★ **Correlating music, history and language skills**

Time Needed:
Approximately 30 minutes

Objective:
Using the facts listed on the worksheet, students will be able to correctly identify the similes in the brief description of Bach.

Materials Needed:
✂ Teacher and student worksheets
✂ Pencils

Lesson:
1. Pass out the worksheets and pencils to the students.
2. Read through the definition of a simile with the class:
    ♪ A simile is a figure of speech which often uses "as" or "like" to compare two unlike things. (Example: My dad is as <u>strong as an ox</u>.)
3. List several other examples of similes on the board:
    ♪ As bold as brass
    ♪ As clear as a bell
    ♪ As tight as a drum
4. Instruct the students to read the story about Bach on their worksheet and underline the similes.
5.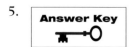

    ♪ sing like a bird
    ♪ as smart as a whip
    ♪ as busy as a bee
    ♪ as lovely as a rose
    ♪ fresh as dew
    ♪ as sweet as honey
    ♪ charming as a prince
    ♪ as blind as a bat
6. Review the answers together when the students have completed the assignment.

Student name _____

Similes

A simile is a figure of speech which often uses "as" or "like" to compare two unlike things. (Example: My dad is <u>as strong as an ox</u>.)

Underline the similes

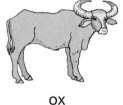

Strong   as an   ox

Johann Sebastian Bach was born into a musical family in Eisenach, Germany on March 21, 1685. His father taught him how to play the violin. Sadly, by the time he was ten years old, both of his parents had died, so he moved in with his older brother. When he was fifteen years old, he was sent to a choir school because he could sing like a bird. Even though his voice matured shortly after he arrived, the monks let him stay because he was as smart as a whip. Not only was he becoming renowned for playing the organ, he was already as busy as a bee composing music for the keyboard and choral works. In 1703, he was hired as the court musician to the Duke's brother in Weimar and worked there for two years. Later he married Maria Barbara Bach who was as lovely as a rose. He got a post in Weimar working for the Duke as a Konzertmeister in 1714. He became famous during this time as both a composer of fine cantatas, which were as fresh as dew and as one of the finest organists in the country. In 1717, Bach was imprisoned by the Duke when he wanted to work elsewhere. He was released after a month. He became the conductor of the court orchestra in Cöthen and wrote his famous Brandenburg Concertos. Unfortunately his first wife died during this time, but a little over a year later he married Anna Magdalena Wilcke, who was as sweet as honey. He wrote numerous light pieces that were charming as a prince for his new wife which were preserved in a notebook. Although Bach was well known for being a virtuoso when it came to playing the organ, he was only acclaimed for his compositions in the immediate area where he lived. During the last years of his life, he became poor and blind as a bat. He died on July 28, 1750 and was buried in an unmarked grave. His musical genius was not truly appreciated by the world until after his death. Today he is commonly referred to as "The Father of Music" and is well known for his hundreds of cantatas, fugues, oratorios and countless works for the church. Several of his sons carried on the family tradition and became outstanding musicians as well (he had twenty children.)

Vocabulary Words

- **Post**: job, a place of employment
- **Konzertmeister**: The first violinist in an orchestra-leader
- **Composer**: A person who writes original music
- **Cantata**: A piece which is sung
- **Concerto**: A work for one or more voices with instrumental accompaniment
- **Virtuoso**: A performer who exhibits superior skills and technical mastery
- **Fugue**: A theme which occurs at the beginning of the piece, then recurs frequently thereafter
- **Oratorio**: the story and lyrics are based on a sacred or epic theme for chorus, soloists and orchestra and usually performed in a church or a concert hall

Math

Although mathematics demonstrates logic and music expresses our emotional nature, we can find many commonalities in both disciplines:

- the musical scale is equally divided into 12 half steps
- pitch intervals are described numerically
- meter signatures are fractions
- note values are quantified, dividing a "whole" into fractions
- "measures" can be described as "sets"
- Roman numerals are used to identify chords
- symbols are used to represent values
- both math and music contain patterns

Fluency in math is defined as students having automatic recall of basic facts. The on-going success of a student can be greatly hindered if fact fluency is not achieved. Using the study of music, students can rehearse math facts using equations including note values, providing additional practice on both math and musical skill fluency. Simulated "musical-math" events can create interest and purpose for such non-musical skills as bar graphing and solving mathematical word problem, too.

Add It Up!

★ **Correlating music and math skills**

Time Needed:
Approximately 3 to 30 minutes

Objective:
By calculating the correct value of two notes, the students will be able to toss the ball to a teammate on the correct beats.

Materials Needed:
✂ Plastic blow-up beach ball

Lesson:
1. Review the value of notes in whatever meter signature you designate.
2. Have the students practice giving you the sum of two notes (ex. $\frac{4}{4}$ time—two half notes would equal 4 beats or a quarter and a half note would equal 3).
3. Game Directions:
   ♪ Instruct the students to stand in a circle.
   ♪ Have the students clap a steady, even beat.
   ♪ The teacher will shout out two different combinations of notes such as quarter/quarter.
   ♪ Because the sum of the two notes equals two, the student who has the ball would then say one/two in beat with the steady even rhythm being clapped, and toss the ball to another student on the second count.
   ♪ Encourage the students to give everyone a turn.
4. This activity can be used as a regular class activity or as a review at the end of class if you have a few extra minutes of time left.
5. Remind the students to keep the beat steady and try not to get faster.

Get Ready! Get Set! Go!

★ **Correlating music with mathematical geometrical shapes**

Time Needed:
Approximately 15 minutes

Objective:
Using the geometrical shapes displayed on the worksheet, students will be able to correctly identify similarly shaped instruments in the classroom.

Materials Needed:
✂ Teacher and student worksheets
✂ Pencils

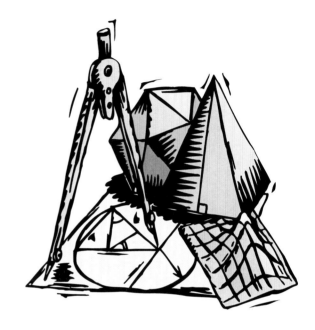

Lesson:
1. Pass out the worksheets and pencils to the students.

2. Review the basic geometrical shapes illustrated on their worksheets.

3. Instruct the students to explore the music classroom and write down as many items as they can find that correspond to the shapes. (Ex. circle/tambourine—triangle/triangle or rectangle/music poster).

4. Allow them 5 to 10 minutes to locate and notate the items.

5. Review as a class at the conclusion of the activity.

   ♪ This activity not only reinforces the names of the geometrical shapes for younger children, it also helps them learn the names of the different instruments and other objects housed in the music classroom.

Student name _____

Get Ready! Get Set! Go!

Get ready to have a little fun! When the teacher instructs you to begin, find as many musical objects in the classroom as you can that are similar to the shapes below. Write the names of the items in the space provided. Good luck!

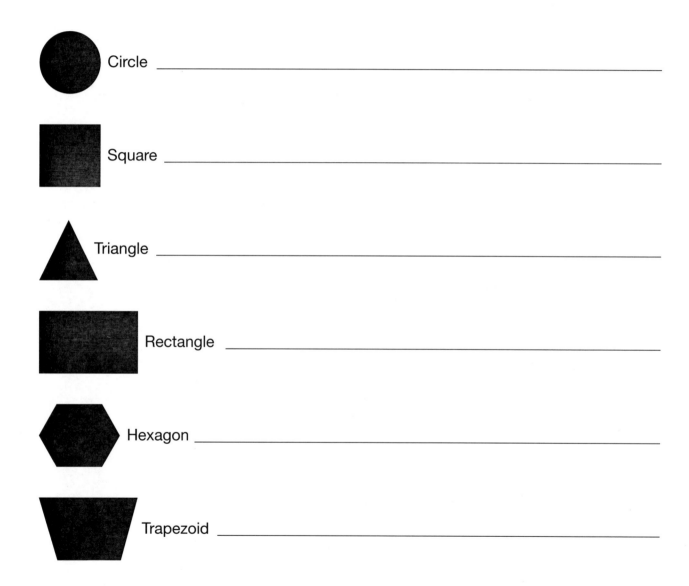

Circle _____

Square _____

Triangle _____

Rectangle _____

Hexagon _____

Trapezoid _____

Maestro Melody's Mysterious Notes

★ **Correlating math and music**

Time Needed:
Approximately 30 minutes

Objective:
The students will be able to incorporate math and logic to solve the musical math problems.

Materials Needed:
✂ Teacher and student worksheets
✂ Pencils

Lesson:
1. Review the values of (♩) quarter note = 1 beat, (♪) half note = 2 beats, (♩.) = dotted half note = 3 beats, and (𝅝) whole note = 4 beats
2. This activity can be completed individually or in small groups. Determine which would be best for your students.
3. Pass out the worksheets and pencils to the students.
4.

    ♪ 1,1,1,2
    ♪ 1,2,3,4
    ♪ whole note
    ♪ 3,2 or 1,4
    ♪ 3,4,5
    ♪ 30

Student name _____

Maestro Melody's Mysterious Notes

Maestro Melody's notes keep mysteriously disappearing and reappearing inside the instruments of the orchestra. Help her solve this problem by using a logical process.

(♩) quarter note = 1 beat (♩) half note = 2 beats

(♩.) dotted half note = 3 beats (o) whole note = 4 beats

1. The Maestro has four drums. Each of the drums contains at least one or more quarter notes. If the sum of the notes is five beats, how many quarter notes are in each of the four drums?
    Answer: _____

2. The Maestro has four saxophones with different amounts of half notes in each instrument. If no saxophone has more than four half notes, how many half notes are in each saxophone?
    Answer: _____

3. The Maestro has two oboes with two equal notes in each instrument. If the sum of the four notes equals sixteen beats, what type of note is in the oboes?
    Answer: _____

4. The Maestro has two string basses with different amounts of dotted half notes in both instruments. If the sum equals fifteen, how many half notes are in each instrument?
    Answer: _____

5. The Maestro has three trumpets with different amounts of quarter notes in each horn. If each instrument has one more note than the one before it and the sum of all the notes equals twelve, how many quarter notes are in each trumpet?
    Answer: _____

6. The Maestro is working with a string quartet. The violin has only quarter notes, the viola has only half notes, the cello has only dotted half notes and the string bass has only whole notes. If each instrument has only three notes, what is the sum of all of the notes?
    Answer: _____

Musical Math Mystery Box

★ **Correlating math and music**

Time Needed:
Approximately 3 plus minutes

Objective:
The students will be able to incorporate math and logic to solve the mystery musical math problems.

Materials Needed:

✂ Shoe box wrapped in pretty musical paper (the lid must be wrapped separately) and topped with a colorful bow.

✂ Unlined index cards with various combinations of notes written on it appropriate to the grade level.

Lesson:

1. Review the values of (♩) quarter note = 1 beat, (♩) half note = 2 beats, (♩.) dotted half note = 3 beats, and (○) whole note = 4 beats

2. Inside the box, place several index cards which have a variety of music notes written on them. Determine what the combined value of the notes equals and notate it on the back of each card.

3. Tell the students what the sum of the notes equals. (Example: 20)

4. The students now have to guess the exact combination of notes you wrote down. (Example: two whole notes, four half notes, and four quarter notes.) Write the wrong combinations on the board so they don't guess them again.

   ♪ The mystery box idea has so many possibilities. It could also be used in conjunction with names of notes, (identify two different places you can find the pitch F using both clefs) or instruments, (name the family from which the instrument belongs, then let them narrow down the search), or composers, (list several hints such as the musical period, genre, etc.) or other elements of music studied within the music classroom.

Rhythmic Requirements!

★ **Correlating music and math skills**

Time Needed:
Approximately 30 to 40 minutes

Objective:
Using the student worksheets, the students will be able to correctly solve the musical mathematical problems using elementary math principals and logic.

Materials Needed:
✂ Teacher and student worksheets
✂ Pencils

Lesson:
1. Pass out the worksheets and pencils to the students.
2. Decide whether the students will be working together in groups of two, or individually.
3. Instruct the students to read the worksheets and use their knowledge of math to solve the problems.
4.
Answer Key
⛏━○

   ♪ The best option would be to purchase the rhythm sticks in a bundle. The cost per pair using this option would be $5.00 as opposed to $5.99 when purchased separately.

   ♪ $65.00

   ♪ $90.50

   ♪ $62.50 (Hint! Be careful on this one! The price of the headless tambourines is already totaled!)

   ♪ Yes, the total bill was $278.00

Item description	number of units:	unit price	price:
rhythm sticks	1 bundle	$60.00	$60.00
hand drums	5	$13.00	$65.00
cowbell	1	$33.50	$33.50
maracas	2	$28.50	$57.00
claves	2	$8.25	$16.50
woodblocks	2	$13.00	$26.00
headless tambourines	2	$10.00	$20.00
Total cost (remember to stay under $300 budget)			$278.00

Student name _____

Rhythmic Requirements!

You are a new music teacher at Dolce Elementary School. There are no rhythm instruments in your classroom and you have been given a $300.00 budget to purchase some for your students. You want to spend the money wisely. Please decide which of the following options would be best for your classroom. (No tax will be added since you will be purchasing these items for a school.)

1. First, you decided that you would like to order 12 pairs of rhythm sticks. You noticed that you could buy them individually for $5.99 a pair or in a bundle which sells 12 pairs of rhythm sticks for $60.

    Which would be the best option? Buying them separately or in the bundle?

    _____

    Why is it the best choice?

    _____

2. You would also like to purchase 5 hand drums. They cost $13.00 a piece.

    How much would the drums cost? _____

3. You would like to add a little pizzazz to the ensemble, so you decide to add a cowbell which costs $33.50, and 2 maracas priced at $28.50 each.

    What is the total of this purchase? _____

4. Finally, you have a brilliant idea! Why not order 2 claves which cost $8.25 each, 2 rhythm woodblocks at $13.00 each, and 2 headless tambourines which total to $20.00 to really shake things up!

    What was the cost of all 6 of these instruments? _____

5. Did you stay within your budget or go over? _____

   What was the total amount that you spent? _____

Item description	number of units:	unit price	price:
rhythm sticks	1 bundle	$60.00	$60.00
hand drums			
cowbell	1	$33.50	$33.50
maracas			
claves			
woodblocks			
headless tambourines			
Total cost (remember to stay under $300 budget)			

Sassy Sudoku

★ **Correlating music and math skills**

Time Needed:
Approximately 1 class period (may be used as an "anchor" activity)

Objective:
Using rhythmic notation, students will solve a Sudoku puzzle.

Materials Needed:
✂ Student worksheets
✂ Pencils

Lesson:
1. Distribute the worksheets and pencils to the students.
2. Discuss the rules of Sudoku (these may be placed on the board):
    ♪ Each 3x3 grid contains the numbers 1–9
    ♪ Each vertical column and row contains the numbers 1–9
    ♪ The numbers may not be repeated in any 3x3 section or any single row
    ♪ In this musical version, the answers must be written in rhythmic notation.
3. Note: this activity may also be used as an "anchor" activity. (A continuing project that students may work on when they have completed their regular differentiated assignments.)

4.

Student name _____

Sassy Sudoku

Instead of placing a number in each square, place the musical combination that is equal to the number in the box. Remember, the numbers may not appear more than once in any row! Have fun!

♩ = 1 beat   ♩+♩+♩ = 4 beats   o+♩+♩ = 7 beats
♩ = 2 beats   ♩.+♩ = 5 beats   o+o = 8 beats
♩. = 3 beat   ♩.+♩. = 6 beats   o+o+♩ = 9 beats

Symphony Board Report

★ **Correlating music and math skills**

Time Needed:
30 minutes

Objective:
Using a "simulated event" and bar graphs, students will identify and categorize orchestral instruments.

Materials Needed:
✂ Teacher and student worksheets
✂ Pencils, crayons, markers, and/or colored pencils, if available

Lesson:
1. Brain researchers have discovered that simulated events or "simulations" increase student recall, since the activity is more like a "real life" event, which creates meaning.

2. This "simulation," puts the student in the role of a Symphony Orchestra office manager, preparing an annual report on the orchestra's membership.

3. Students will read the directions and complete the bar graphs for their "share holders annual report."

4. 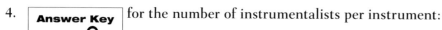 for the number of instrumentalists per instrument:

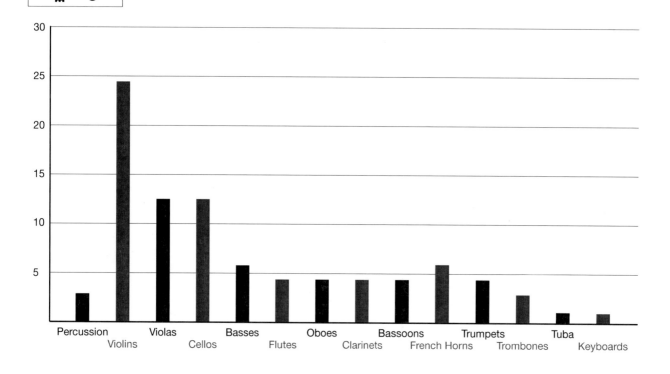

5. **Answer Key** for the number of instrumentalists per instrument:

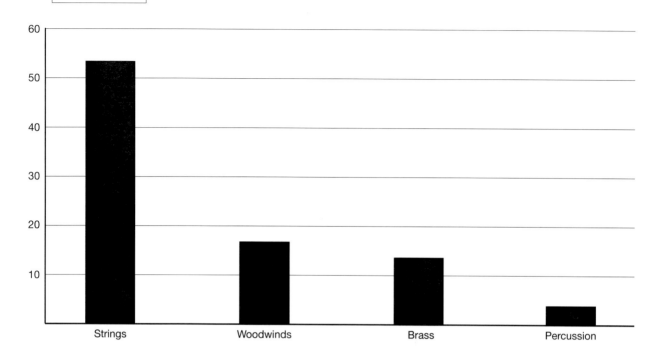

Annual Symphony Board Report

Scenario: You serve as the office manager of a major symphony orchestra. Each year, you are required to submit reports to the symphony board which will help plan their budget for salaries and propose the size of space needed for rehearsals and performances. Complete the graphs, neatly and accurately.

Here are the staffing numbers you need to complete your report:

- 3 Percussionists
- 24 violinists
- 12 violists
- 12 cellists
- 6 bassists
- 4 flutists
- 4 oboists
- 4 clarinetists
- 4 bassoonists
- 6 French hornists
- 4 trumpeters
- 3 trombonists
- 1 tubist
- 1 keyboardist (note: the piano is classified as a percussion instrument)

When you have completed the bar graphs, sign the report (as the symphony office manager) before submitting it to your teacher (the board president).

Date: _____

Annual Staff Report

Dear Symphony Board Members,

Below, you will find a bar graph of our symphony staff, categorized by instrument. Our upcoming season will include *The Young Person's Guide to the Orchestra*, written by Benjamin Britten, which will feature each section of the orchestra.

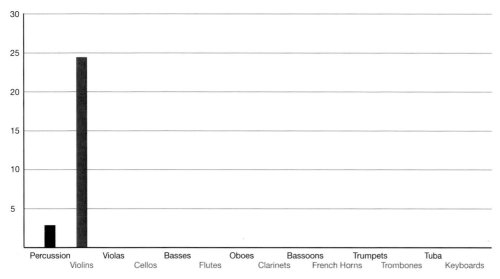

Here is an overview of the number of instruments currently staffing each section of our orchestra:

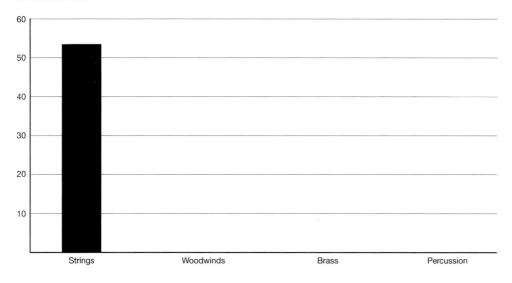

Respectfully submitted:

_____, Symphony Office Manager

Two Plus Two

★ **Correlating math and music**

Time Needed:
Approximately 3 to 5 minutes

Objective:
The students will be able to add the values of musical notes together.

Materials Needed:
✂ Music Flash Cards

Lesson:
1. This activity can be used effectively if you have a few extra moments at the end of class.
2. Review the values of (♩) quarter note = 1 beat, (♩) half note = 2 beats, (♩.) dotted half note = 3 beats, and (o) whole note = 4 beats
3. Rules of the game:
   - ♪ Ask the students to form two lines (teams).
   - ♪ Form the lines so all students can see the flash cards (to keep them engaged).
   - ♪ Select a student to flash two different cards at the first two "players" in the beginning of their lines.
   - ♪ The first student to correctly add the two combinations of notes wins a point for their team (line).
   - ♪ If another student, other than the first two players, reveals the answer before the two players answer (correctly or incorrectly), the opposite team wins the point.
   - ♪ If neither student is able to answer correctly, then a student from the line may "steal" the answer to earn a bonus point (engaging all students even when it isn't their "turn").
   - ♪ The first correct answer receives the point (if multiple correct answers are stated simultaneously, both teams will receive a point).
   - ♪ After each question, the first two students walk to the end of the line so everyone can have a turn.
   - ♪ The student in charge of the cards selects two new note values.
   - ♪ Use the first set of cards for primary grades and the second set for intermediate grades.

Cards for Primary Grade Levels

Copy the notes below—make extra copies for additional cards. Cut, glue onto heavy weight paper or note cards, and laminate.

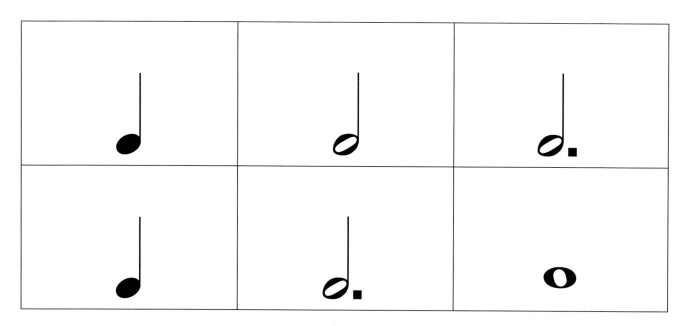

Cards for Intermediate Grade Levels

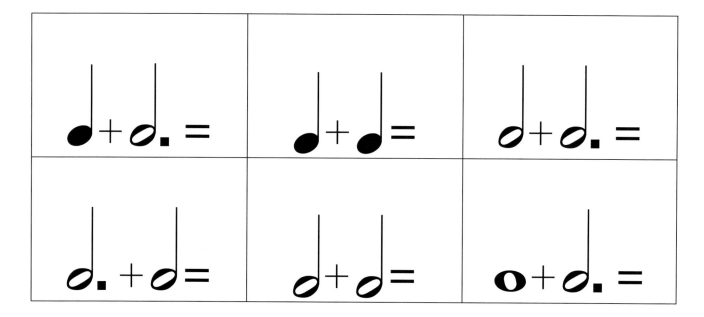

Commercial Calculations

★ **Correlating math and music**

Time Needed:
Approximately 30 minutes

Objective:
Using mathematical equations, students solve simulated musical events.

Materials Needed:
✂ Student worksheets
✂ Pencils
✂ Metronome (free metronome found at metronomeonline.com)

Lesson:
1. Discuss the qualifications of a commercial composer:
   - ♪ Must be able to compose short, "catchy" pieces of music with specific moods.
   - ♪ Must have an understanding of music notation software, how to score for different instruments, and how to complete mathematical equations accurately to determine the exact length needed for theme songs and jingles.
2. Pass out the worksheets and pencils.
3. Read the Italian tempo markings and demonstrate ranges of tempi (Largo – Presto).
4. Students complete the worksheets.
5.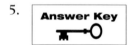

   - ♪ 128 beats per minute (multiply 64 x 2, since the segment is 30 seconds long)
   - ♪ "Allegro" (120–139 beats per minute)
   - ♪ Four phrases (16 x 4 = 64)
   - ♪ Two phrases (Divide the commercial in half.)
   - ♪ Same tempo
   - ♪ 192 beats per minute (multiply 64 x 3, since the segment is 20 seconds long)
   - ♪ "Presto" (176–200 beats per minute)

Student name _____

Commercial Calculations

Largo (very slow) = 40 to 60 bpm (beats per minute)   **Adagio** (slow) = 66 to 76 bpm
Andante (a walking speed) = 76 to 108 bpm   **Moderato** (medium speed) = 108 to 116 bpm
Allegro (fast) = 120 to 139 bpm   **Presto** (very fast) = 176 to 200 bpm

You are a composer and need to create background music for a funny car insurance television commercial. The "tempo" (or speed of the beat) needs to be fast and cheerful to suit the mood of the actors and the action in the advertisement. You have exactly 30 seconds of time to fill and you have to decide how many beats per minute you will need.

1. You've counted the number of beats in your composition and found out there are a total of 64 beats. How many beats per minute would you need to make your composition fit exactly within the 30 second commercial? _____ beats per minute.

2. If you wrote the Italian term (as a tempo direction) at the beginning of your piece, which term would you write? _____

3. Musical sentences are called "phrases." If each phrase of your commercial is the same length, how many phrases of 16 counts are in your composition?
_____

4. The advertisement agency wants you to do a 15 second version of your commercial theme for the radio. How many phrases can you do in that amount of time without increasing the tempo? _____

5. Can you keep the same tempo for the radio commercial, or do you have to perform it faster or slower? _____

   Next, you've been asked to write and perform a television theme song. The show is a reality show, featuring a family of recyclers. The theme song you've written is a quick-paced, tongue twister entitled, "Reduce, Reuse, Recycle."

6. If the theme song, "Reduce, Reuse, Recycle," is only 20 seconds and you have 64 beats of music to perform, how many beats per minute will your theme have?
_____

7. Which Italian tempo would you use for "Reduce, Reuse, Recycle?" _____

Science

Science is the study of observable facts, which can be tested for validity by other "scientists" working under the same conditions. The study of music intersects the science world by its very nature: sound properties. Sound vibrations, affecting pitch, timbre, and volume are intriguing to "would-be scientists," creating excellent opportunities to discuss instrument tone production and characteristics of musical instrument tone quality, while they grab the attention of non-musical learners.

Connecting your music class to the science lab through musical improvisations, based on the rhythm of scientific vocabulary, rehearses important language and concepts, while students create phrasing, lyrics, and form to construct a meaning musically experience.

Composed, science-related songs and musicals also provide additional opportunities for "singing, alone and with others, a varied repertoire of music," as well as, an entertaining event for peer or parent performance! (What a great way to let your clientele know that you're *Teaching Music Across the Curriculum*!)

Science Improvisations

★ **Vocabulary used as lyrics**

Time Needed:
Approximately 40 minutes

Objective:
The students will create a musical improvisation using vocabulary from any curricular topic (including Italian music vocabulary)

Materials Needed:
✂ Orff Instrumentarium (Pentatonic scale: C, D, E, G, A—remove **fa** and **ti** , if possible)
✂ Dry Erase Board/markers

Lesson:
1. Ask the students to name a non-music curriculum topic they are studying in their classroom from one of the following topics:
   ♪ Communication Arts
   ♪ Math
   ♪ Social Studies/History
   ♪ Science

2. Allowing students to choose the topic increases "ownership" and hooks the students into the lesson emotionally.
   ♪ Students sometimes demonstrate their misunderstanding of important vocabulary and this discussion provides you, the music teacher, an opportunity to "correct" or reinforce correct information.

3. Choose a curricular topic, such as *"Water Cycle"* and ask the students to describe the process using vocabulary words from that subject.
   ♪ **Groundwater** is water beneath the surface of the ground.
   ♪ **Water Table** is the surface of groundwater.
   ♪ **Condensation** is gas turning into liquid.
   ♪ **Evaporation** is liquid turning into a gas (the antonym of Condensation).
   ♪ **Precipitation** is condensation from clouds, in the form of rain, snow, hail, sleet, and freezing rain.

4. Write the vocabulary words on the dry erase board.

5. Identify rhythmic patterns, using the vocabulary words and phrases, to create short patterns.

6. Clap the rhythm patterns and/or write the rhythm patterns on the board.

7. Depending upon the level and ability of the group:

♪ Make the patterns short and easy to remember

♪ Give students input on the rhythms

8. The students will use specific rhythm patterns using the Pentatonic scale (do, re, mi, sol, la) or C, D, E, G, A (in the key of "C").

   ♪ Provide opportunity for supervised rehearsal of the patterns.

   ♪ Remind students to perform "musically"—this particular activity can be a "gentle rain" (not a "hurricane").

9. Instruct students they will be performing "solos" and "ensemble" parts using the following pattern:

   ♪ Select four Bass Xylophone and Metallophone performers to create an ostinato (bourdon) on the pitches C and G.

   ♪ The performers will apply the vocabulary word *"Groundwater"* (Ta-ah, Ta, Ta).

   ♪ Two performers per instrument

   ♪ Hint: The example uses harmonic intervals, but if you have limited number of mallets, use **melodic intervals**, such as C, G, G, to perform with one mallet per performer.

   ♪ Alto Xylophone performers will apply the vocabulary words *"Water table"* (Ta, Ta, Ta, Ta), performing their improvisation on pitches: G, E, G, E (sol, mi, sol, mi)

   ♪ Two performers per instrument

   ♪ Soprano Xylophone performers will apply the vocabulary word *"Condensation"* (Ta, Ta, Ta, Ta), performing their improvisation on pitches: G, E, G, E (sol, mi, sol, mi).

     • Two performers per instrument

   ♪ Alto Metallophone performers will apply the vocabulary word *"Evaporation"* (Ta, ti, ti, Ta, Ta), performing their improvisation on pitches: C, D, E, G, A (the pentatonic scale).

     • Two performers per instrument

     • Ask: "Which direction should the melody for 'Evaporation' move? (Upward)

     • Demonstrate an upward melodic movement (going from C–A)

     • Students may vary the melody (using repeated or some lower pitches), but the melody should general move upward

   ♪ Soprano Metallophone players will apply the vocabulary word *"Precipitation"* (Ta, Ti Ti, Ta, Ta), performing their improvisation on pitches: C, D, E, G, A (the pentatonic scale).

     • Two performers per instrument

     • Ask: "Which direction should the melody for 'Precipitation' move?" (Downward)

     • Demonstrate a downward melodic movement (going from A–C).

     • Students may vary the melody (using repeated or some higher pitches), but it should generally move downward.

   ♪ Tone chimes (if available) will again use the pentatonic scale. Students will choose two pitches from the pentatonic scale (C, D, E, G, A) and with alternate hands (left/right), play our topic: *"Water Cycle"* (Ta, Ta, Ta, Ta)

     • This provides a full harmonization to the piece, but also requires students to listen for balance with the other parts.

   ♪ Provide feedback to help students experience a "musical" experience:

     • No harsh playing

     • Pulse of the music is very steady (don't rush)

- Everyone is playing their rhythm patterns correctly
- Listen for balance between parts

♪ Before combining the entire ensemble, perform each element separately, to verify students understand their individual parts and everyone can hear all parts.

- Students will eventually switch parts and peer demonstration is an extremely valuable tool

♪ After everyone is secure on their parts, perform the following "RONDO" pattern (A, B, A, C, A, D, A, E, A, F, A).

♪ Write the pattern on the board, labeling each section as follows, clarifying and labeling each section as it is written:

- **A section** will be the entire ensemble for 16 beats .
- **B section** will be the Bass Xylophone and Metallophone (16 beats playing "Groundwater").
- Ask: "If the whole group plays their part again, which letter should we use?" (A) Label the next section as the A section (entire ensemble – 16 beats).
- **C section** will be Alto Xylophone (16 beats playing "Water Table") and the Soprano Xylophone (16 beats playing "Condensation"); notice both parts are identical (rhythm and pitch), even though they are using two different vocabulary words.
- **A section** (entire ensemble – 16 beats)
- **D section** will be the Alto Metallophone (16 beats playing "Evaporation")
- **A section** (entire ensemble – 16 beats)
- **E section** will be the Soprano Metallophone (16 beats playing "Precipitation")
- **A section** (entire ensemble – 16 beats)
- **F section** will be the tone chimes (16 beats playing "Water Cycle")
- "We finish our pattern with the **A section**" (entire ensemble – 16 beats)

10. Practice the rondo, using the vocabulary to reinforce the improvisation's rhythm.

11. Include **dynamics** to make it sound more musical, while reinforcing phrasing and each section's form.

12. The example provided will give you, the teacher, an idea of type of patterns to expect from your students. Since this is an improvisation, practice the rhythmic patterns, but allow for variation with the melodic direction.

♪ As students become more sophisticated, their improvisations will begin to sound musical and they'll be able to play very successfully as an ensemble.

♪ With larger classes, ask additional students to serve as "coaches" and help make certain their "player" is performing their improvisation correctly (switch places and the "player" becomes the "coach").

Water Cycle

Lyrics by Greg Foreman

Improvisation

Tell Me Why!

★ **Correlating music and science skills**

Time Needed:
Approximately 40 minutes

Objective:
Using the facts written on the worksheet, the students will gain an understanding of the basic principles of sound.

Materials Needed:
✂ Teacher and student worksheets
✂ Tuning fork
✂ 1 balloon per student
✂ Xylophone (or any other barred instrument)

Lesson:
1. Distribute the worksheets to the students.
2. Read the introduction on the worksheet together as a class.
3. Perform the Get Ready! Get Set! Go! Demonstration.
    ♪ Before the students begin their race, have the class vote on who the winner will be.
4. Ask the class why the second runner was the winner. (Because he/she didn't have as far to run, the runner could cover the distance far more quickly!)
5. Now let's try another experiment! Tuning fork magic! Have one of the students read the brief paragraph describing this experiment, then strike the tuning fork against something hard, and place the end of the fork on the small bone in front of each student's earlobes. They will react in amazement when they can hear the pitch caused from the vibrations.
6. Perform the final experiment — Furiously Fast and Super Slow Vibrations!
    ♪ Place a xylophone, or other barred instrument, in an area that all the students can easily see the bars.
    ♪ Read through the introductory paragraph with the students.
    ♪ Ask the students to predict if the largest bar or the smallest bar will have the lowest pitch. (*The largest bar will have the lowest pitch because the slower the vibrations travel, the lower the pitch will be. Likewise, the faster the vibrations travel, the higher the pitch will be. *The vibrations had to cover a larger area which slowed down the vibrations!*)
7. Instruct the students to fill out the reflection questions at the end of the student sheet.
8.
Answer Key

    ♪ Sounds are made from vibrations.
    ♪ The man because he's bigger (more mass).
    ♪ The smaller drum has the higher pitch because it has a smaller surface area to cover.
    ♪ The larger gong will have the lower pitch because it has a larger area to cover.

Tell Me!
A Science Connection: Pitch/Vibrations

When you're singing a song, have you ever noticed that the pitches in the melody are not all the same? Although a few of the pitches may repeat; the other pitches generally move up and down in different patterns to form a melody. How do we make these pitches? Sound! Sound is caused by vibrations passing through the air! Let's try an experiment!

Tuning Fork Magic

Can vibrations really make sound? Let's find out. Your teacher is going to strike a tuning fork which will cause it to vibrate, and then place it on the small bone right under your ear. Could you hear a pitch made from the vibrations?

Get Ready! Get Set! Go!

Your teacher is going to stand two students behind a starting line. Student #1 has to run the length of the room and back 3 times. Student #2 only has to run 5 feet and back 3 times. Let's make a prediction. Who will finish first?

Furiously Fast and Super Slow Vibrations

The faster the vibrations – the higher the pitch!

The slower the vibrations – the lower the pitch!

Let's get a xylophone. Look at the bars very carefully. Will the long bars have a higher or lower pitch than the smaller bars? Strike the mallet on the lowest bar and then the highest bar. Which had the lowest pitch?

"Singing Balloons"

Your teacher is going to give each of you a balloon to blow up and tie the bottom into a knot. When your teacher gives you permission, hold the balloon very closely to your lips and sing loudly. What do you feel? The vibrations from the sound not only vibrate the balloon, but you can feel the vibrations in your lips too! Notice that when you sing higher pitches, the vibrations are faster than when you sing lower pitches.

Student name _____

Your Turn to Tell Me!

1. Sounds are made from _____

2. If a large man and a small boy each cannon balled into a pool, which person would make the most vibrations in the water? The man or the boy? _____

3. Circle the drum that has the highest pitch?

   Tell me what causes the effect of higher pitch?

   _____

   _____

   _____

   _____

4. Circle the gong with the lowest pitch.

   Tell me what causes the effect of lower pitch?

   _____

   _____

   _____

   _____

The Rainbow Race

★ **Music and Science correlation**

Time Needed:
Several class periods

Objective:
The students will gain an understanding of the formation of rainbows using a play format.

Materials Needed:
✂ Teacher and student worksheets
✂ Song sheets

Lesson:
1. Distribute both the worksheets and the song sheets to the students.
2. Read through the play with the class.
3. Teach the songs from the play.
4. Assign cast parts:
   ♪ Malia – Friend
   ♪ Destiny – Leader of the girls
   ♪ Melody – Whiner
   ♪ Chase – Friend
   ♪ Geoff – Friend
   ♪ Cody – Friend
   ♪ Albert – The Brain
   ♪ Chorus
5. Perform the play for each other or another class.

The Rainbow Race

Girls enter stage R – Boys enter stage L – the students are carrying various school items (i.e. books, lunchboxes, etc.) Students meet center stage.

Malia: Hi Cody! Hi Chase! Hi Albert!

Chase & Geoff: Hi!

Destiny: This must be my lucky day! Check out that gorgeous rainbow! It's a sign! Good luck is on my way!

Cody: Cool!

Albert: Destiny, I'm glad you enjoy the spectrum of colors produced by a rainbow, but I fail to see how that image could possibly affect your luck! Long ago, people used to be afraid of rainbows, thinking they were snakes that rose up into the sky to drink water. Some superstitious people even warned that you should never point at a rainbow or you could lose your finger! But we have long since discovered that these silly beliefs were groundless myths. Unfortunately for you, there is also no conclusive evidence that links rainbows to that ever evasive quality known as luck!

Melody: (Whining) Oh Albert! Must you always be so literal? Rainbows are just plain fun.

Chase: I'm in the mood for a little fun. I challenge you and your little girly friends to a race. Let's just see who can get to the end of that rainbow first. We might even find a pot of gold! Meet back here in thirty minutes!

Malia: You're on!

Boys run stage R – Girls run stage L

Geoff: It looks like the rainbow starts over in that direction, but it's kind of hard to tell where it ends.

Chase: Do you have any ideas, oh wise one?

Albert: As a matter of fact, I do. Here come the girls! Let's move to a more neutral area so we can devise a plan.

Boys run off stage – Girls move center stage

Pam: Did you see the way the boys took off? I think we're getting close.

Christy: But they're still ahead of us and they have the smartest boy in the class with them, Albert!

Melody: (Whining) We don't stand a chance! I'm tired. My feet hurt from all of this running around. I wanna go back to school. This is a stupid contest anyway!

Denise: Don't be such a quitter! We're girls! We'll find a way.

Malia: All we have to do is to pool our brainpower.

Destiny: I don't want to brag or anything, but I'm kind of an expert on rainbows myself. They're sooooo romantic! It's all about "The Colors of Love."

Sing "The Colors of Love." Girls begin, then boys join them singing the Soprano 2 part.

The Colors of Love (Für Elise)

Lyrics by Valerie Luppens

Adapted (Beethoven)

Cody: Hey guys. Do you think we're getting any closer to the rainbow?

Chase: Probably, but we've only been walking for fifteen minutes.

Geoff: We're definitely getting closer. The colors look different now.

Albert: I hate to disillusion you, but from the top edge of the rainbow to the bottom, the order of the colors is always red, orange, yellow green, blue, indigo and violet. Also, the brightness of the colors and their width may change from one minute to the next and from one rainbow to another. Therefore, your assumption is once more based on misinformation.

Robert: So are you saying we're no closer now than when we started?

Albert: I think that's a safe assumption, Robert.

Girls rejoin the boys center stage

Destiny: Hi guys! Did you find the end of the rainbow yet?

Boys: See ya! Bye!

Boys exit

Malia: What's their problem?

Christy: Obviously they're afraid we're going to win.

Pam: We need to move faster or they will win!

Melody: (Whining) Noooo! I'm thirsty! Let's give it up. You don't really think we have a chance of finding it, do you?

Melody sings "Give It Up", followed by Girls singing "We Can Win"

Give It Up!

Adapted from Rossini's
"William Tell Overture"

Give it up! Give it up! Give it

up right now! Turn a - round! Turn a - round! I'll show you how! We can

win! We can win! We just don't know how! And this tor - ture I just won't al - low!

We Can Win!

Adapted from Rossini's
"William Tell Overture"

We can win! We can win! We just

have to try! We won't stop! 'Til we drop! We can beat the guys! We are

smart! We are smart and we're oh, so sly! Let's go find____ the rain-bow in the sky!

Teaching Music Across the Curriculum

Girls exit stage after song – boys enter

Cody: Guys, I hate to tell you this, but we're running out of time fast.

Robert: Yeah, we only have about four minutes left before we have to meet the girls.

Chase: But we haven't found the end of the rainbow yet!

Geoff: No pot of gold for us. We didn't get close!

Albert: For your information, over 2000 years ago, the famous Greek scholar Aristotle said a rainbow is not an object we can touch in space. Instead, it is a series of places in the sky where we see light spread out or scattered. This occurrence depends on where we are standing in relation to the sun. As we move about, a rainbow tags along with us, just as the moon seems to follow us as we walk. So you see, this venture has been hopeless from the beginning.

Geoff: Why didn't you tell us that in the first place?

Albert: You didn't ask!

Girls join the boys on stage

Chase: Here come the girls again. We might as well all go back together.

Robert: We're giving up. Want to call it quits?

Malia: No, but thanks for asking. We've got a couple of minutes yet. I think we'll keep trying.

Melody: (Whining) Are you sure? I'm hot and I'm thirsty!

Denise: Just a few more minutes. I think we're getting close.

Girls exit stage again

Cody: You don't think they'll find anything do you?

Albert: Of course not! Have you ever known me to be wrong?

Geoff: Let's go get a drink, then we can make fun of the girls when they come back for not having the sense to quit earlier.

Guys exit – Girls return

Destiny: Listen to this! According to our science book, it says the higher above the ground you are when viewing a rainbow, the more of the rainbow circle you can see. In fact, from an airplane in flight, a rainbow will appear as a complete circle with the shadow of the airplane in the center.

Pam: And your point?

Christy: We need to get up high to see the rainbow better. We have just enough time to run to the top of that hill over there and take a look. What have we got to lose?

Girls run around the auditorium – find the hidden pot of gold and return to the stage where the boys are now waiting. Girls greet the boys with excited shouts

Girls: We win! We win! We found the pot of gold!

Albert: Impossible!

Geoff: I don't believe it!

Pam: See for yourself!

Christy: Here it is!

Albert: These aren't real golden coins! They're chocolates wrapped in gold paper! I should have known!

Denise: It's still a treasure to us! The candy's quite yummy. And look at this. There's a coupon good for one free wish!

Melody: (Whining) I don't want the wish or the candy! If I eat chocolate it will make me thirsty and we don't have anything to drink here. Then my throat will get sore. I just hate it when I feel parched. And if I made a wish, I'd always be worried that I could have wished for something even better! The pressure! I just can't take it. All I want to do is to go home now. Can you at least grant me that simple wish?

Destiny: I sure can and I also have the perfect wish which will make everyone so much happier. I wish Melody would stop whining!

Everyone: Yes!

Melody: Wellllll! All you had to do was to ask me. I don't see why you're making such a big fuss over such a little thing. I promise I won't whine anymore!

Everyone except Melody sing "Hallelujah!"

Hallelujah "Chorus"

Adapted from Handel's Messiah

Hal - le - lu - jah!

Hal - le - lu - jah! Hal-le - lu - jah! Hal-le-lu - jah! Hal - le - lu - jah!

Shoebox Guitar

★ **Correlating music with science**

Time Needed:
Approximately 1 class period

Objective:
The students will construct a shoebox guitar to gain an understanding of how the frequency of vibrations affects pitch.

Materials Needed:
✂ 1 shoebox per student
✂ 1 box cutter
✂ 1 – 21 inch paint stirrer (available free at most paint stores)
✂ Scissors
✂ 4 Rubber bands that vary in thickness for each guitar
✂ Decorative duck tape in various colors and designs (Students can bring their own in if desired)
✂ Stickers (optional)
✂ Colored Sharpie pens (optional)
✂ Pencil, ink pen, crayon, or construction toys to create a "Bridge" (optional)

Lesson:
1. Prior to teaching:
   ♪ Visit a paint store and ask the owners to donate stirrers for the shoebox project.
   ♪ Have each student bring 1 shoebox to class marked with their name and their teacher's name inside the box.
   ♪ Tell the students that if they wish to decorate their shoebox guitar with any special stickers or tape, they can bring additional supplies from home and store the items inside their marked box.
   ♪ Ask several parent volunteers to come in and cut a 3½ inch circle in the middle of each box and a slit in the lower middle section of one of the sides of the box to insert the stirrer into.

2. Instruct the students:
   ♪ Insert the stirrer into the side of the box.
   ♪ Decorate their boxes and stirrer.
   ♪ Wrap 4 different width rubber bands around the box.
   ♪ Pluck each band to determine which "string" had the higher pitch.
   ♪ (Hint! Create an optional "bridge" using a pen, colored pencil, crayon, etc.)

3. Discuss why the bands have varying pitch:
   ♪ The rubber band that was the thinnest vibrated faster and had a higher frequency, resulting in a higher pitch.

♪ Likewise, the rubber band that was the widest vibrated the slowest and had a lower frequency, resulting in a lower pitch.

Easy as 1–2–3

#1 Insert the stirrer into your pre-cut box

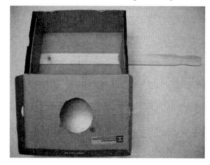

#2 Decorate your box

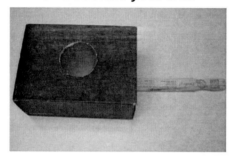

#3 Wrap rubber bands around decorated guitar

About the Authors

Valeaira Luppens served as an elementary music specialist in the Lee's Summit, Missouri School District for 21 years. She is a recipient of the "Expect the Best" award, a district-wide honor for exemplary teaching and service. The award encompasses all disciplines and is awarded to one outstanding staff member, monthly. Valearia earned her Bachelor of Music Education from Central Missouri State University and her Master of Educational Psychology in Research with an emphasis in Gifted/Talented studies from Kansas University. She has belonged to Music Educators National Conference (MENC) throughout her teaching experience and received her certification from the American Orff-Schulwerk Association.

Gregory Foreman holds a Certificate of Piano Performance, a Bachelor of Music Education, a Master of Arts in Teaching, and has completed forty-five post-graduate hours in instructional technology integration and differentiated instruction. He is a member of MENC: The National Association for Music Education, and has been an elementary music specialist since 1984. He has also served as a Lead Teacher for the Lee's Summit's Music Department, "Music in Education" keyboard lab facilitator, mentor teacher, professional staff development affiliate, technology team chair, building web manager, adjudicator, and director of various children's choirs. Greg is the recipient of the "Excellence in Teaching," "Hertzog Leadership," and "Learning for Life" awards, and has performed as soloist with the Kansas City Symphony, the UMKC Conservatory Orchestra, the Youth Symphony of Kansas City, as well as on both National and Kansas Public Radio. He performs regularly at the Kansas City Music Hall and accompanies silent films annually at the Kansas Silent Film Festival, held at Washburn University, Topeka, Kansas.

Notes

Notes